W9-AXA-900

Clownfish

and Other Saltwater Aquarium Fish

Editorial:
Editor in Chief: Paul A. Kobasa
Project Manager: Cassie Mayer
Writer: Ana Deboo
Researcher: Cheryl Graham
Manager, Contracts & Compliance
  (Rights & Permissions): Loranne K. Shields
Indexer: David Pofelski

Graphics and Design:
Manager: Tom Evans
Coordinator, Design Development and
  Production: Brenda B. Tropinski
Senior Designer: Don DiSante
Cartographer: John Rejba

Pre-Press and Manufacturing:
Director: Carma Fazio
Manufacturing Manager:
  Steven K. Hueppchen
Production/Technology Manager:
  Anne Fritzinger

For information about other World Book publications, visit our Web site at http://www.worldbookonline.com or call 1-800-WORLDBK (967-5325).

For information about sales to schools and libraries, call 1-800-975-3250 (United States), or 1-800-837-5365 (Canada).

World Book, Inc.
233 N. Michigan Avenue
Chicago, IL 60601
U.S.A.

Library of Congress Cataloging-in-Publication Data
Clownfish and other saltwater aquarium fish.
    p. cm. -- (World Book's animals of the world)
  Includes index.
  Summary: "An introduction to clownfish and other popular saltwater aquarium fish, presented in a highly illustrated, question-and-answer format. Features include fun facts, glossary, resource list, index, and scientific classification list"--Provided by publisher.
  ISBN 978-0-7166-1374-9
  1. Anemonefishes--Juvenile literature. 2. Marine aquarium fishes--Juvenile literature. I. World Book, Inc.
SF458.A45C56 2010
639.34'2--dc22
                                                2009022480

World Book's Animals of the World
Set 6: ISBN: 978-0-7166-1365-7
Printed in China by Leo Paper Products LTD., Heshan, Guangdong
1st printing November 2009

Picture Acknowledgments: Cover: © Dreamstime; © Peter Leahy, Dreamstime; © Seapics; © Roberto Nistri, Alamy Images; © Asther Lau Choon Siew, Dreamstime.

© Mike Harrington, Alamy Images 61; © Juniors Bildarchiv/Alamy Images 27; © Natural Visions/Alamy Images 29; © Roberto Nistri, Alamy Images 45; © Paul Prescott, Alamy Images 21; © Vario Images/Alamy Images 31; © Dreamstime 3, 4, 5, 15, 17, 33, 37, 41, 43, 47, 59, 62; © iStockphoto 39; © Dorling Kindersley 23; © Dominic Barnardt, Getty Images 7; © Paul Loven, Getty Images 5, 25; © Doug Miannay 57; © Spencer Grant, PhotoEdit 9; © Disney/Pixar/ZUMA Press 55; © Seapics 15, 19, 35; © Shutterstock 15, 49, 53; © Corbis/Superstock 51.

Illustrations: WORLD BOOK illustration by Roberta Polfus 11

World Book's Animals of the World

Clownfish
and Other Saltwater Aquarium Fish

WORLD
BOOK

a Scott Fetzer company
Chicago
www.worldbookonline.com

Contents

What Are Saltwater Aquarium Fish?

An aquarium *(uh KWAIR ee uhm)* is a place where people keep fish and other water animals. Most people who keep aquariums choose fish that live in fresh water, but many people have saltwater, or marine, aquariums. The fish in these aquariums originally came from the ocean. The majority of the fish in saltwater aquariums are native to the warm, shallow waters along the coasts of tropical countries, especially around coral reefs.

Tropical marine fish are popular with experienced aquarists (people who keep aquariums) because of their amazing variety. Many tropical fish are brightly colored, with exciting patterns and interestingly shaped bodies.

In the 1980's, clownfish became the first marine aquarium fish to be bred in quantities large enough to be sold commercially—that is, sold to pet stores and similar businesses. Many aquarists consider them good fish for saltwater aquariums because their care is more straightforward than that of other tropical fish.

A saltwater aquarium

Is a Saltwater Aquarium Right for Your Family?

Saltwater aquariums are more difficult to maintain than freshwater ones, so they are recommended for only experienced aquarists. If no one in your family has ever kept an aquarium, it is best to start with freshwater fish.

Saltwater aquariums require daily care to ensure the environment is suitable for your fish. They are also expensive to set up and maintain—there are many pieces of equipment you will need to keep things running smoothly. An adult or young adult will need to learn testing procedures and spend time on maintenance and cleaning, so the job will be easier if everyone in your family helps out.

In addition, you will need patience when setting up your aquarium. The water must sit for a few weeks before you add fish. Then, fish must be introduced slowly and carefully to make sure they settle in comfortably.

Before your family sets up a saltwater aquarium, be sure everyone is on board with this difficult but rewarding project.

Fish at a pet store

9

What Does a Clownfish Look Like?

Most species (kinds) of clownfish are orange, red, or yellow. They often have white or black markings along the body, or a combination of these colors. The common clownfish is orange with white stripes outlined with a thin black line. The largest clownfish grow from 4 to 6 ½ inches (10 to 17 centimeters) long.

Clownfish have many features in common with other fish. All fish have a backbone, which supports the body. A fish's body is covered with scales—bony plates that protect the body. Fish also have other body parts that help them live in the water. These include fins, which they use for swimming and for balance, and gills, which they use to breathe oxygen in the water.

The shape of a fish's body and other traits are determined by the life it leads. For example, fish that swim fast for long distances may have bullet-shaped bodies. Clownfish almost always stay in a small area, so their bodies are less streamlined.

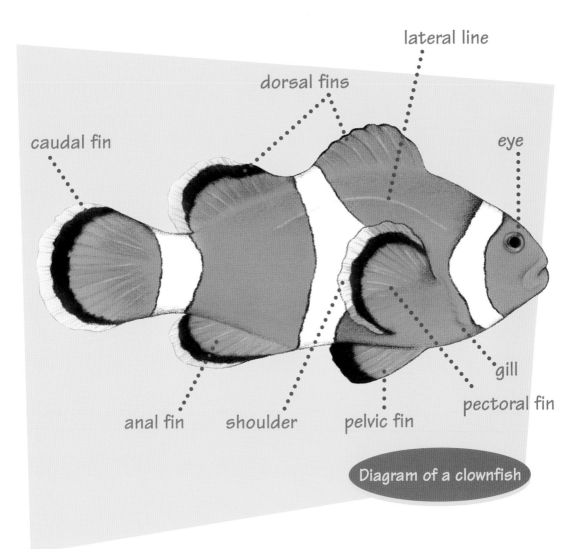

lateral line

dorsal fins

caudal fin

eye

anal fin

shoulder

pelvic fin

gill

pectoral fin

Diagram of a clownfish

Where Do Clownfish Live in the Wild?

Wild clownfish live in coral reefs in the Pacific and Indian oceans. A coral reef is a structure made by tiny animals called corals. The corals attach themselves to the sea floor in groups, or colonies. When they die, their skeletons pile up and slowly change to limestone (a rocky material). Many fish and other sea creatures make their home in coral reefs.

Clownfish typically hide among sea anemones *(uh NEHM uh nees)*—colorful sea animals that resemble flowering plants. In fact, clownfish are also called anemonefish because their relationship to these animals is so important to their survival.

Sea anemones have stinging cells on their tentacles (feelers), but clownfish are coated with a kind of mucus (slimy substance) that protects them. Other fish can't go near the tentacles of an anemone, so clownfish are safe there from hunting animals. Clownfish help sea anemones by eating wastes and parasites that might bother them. They also scare away attackers and give bits of food to their anemone host.

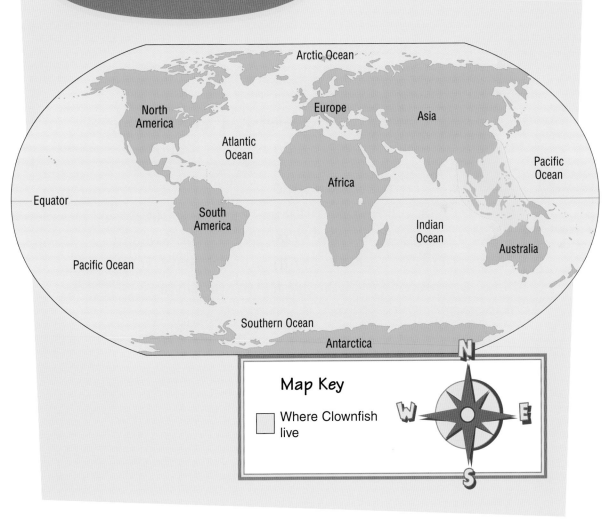

Map showing areas of the ocean where clownfish live.

Arctic Ocean

North America

Europe

Asia

Atlantic Ocean

Pacific Ocean

Africa

Equator

South America

Indian Ocean

Pacific Ocean

Australia

Southern Ocean

Antarctica

Map Key

Where Clownfish live

N
W
E
S

13

What Are Different Kinds of Clownfish?

There are 28 known species of clownfish. Some species are named for the region where they are from, such as the Barrier Reef clownfish, the Australian clownfish, and the Chagos clownfish. Others have names that match their appearance. For example, the skunk clownfish has a white stripe running across the top of its body. The tomato clownfish is dark orange or red.

Several species of clownfish are available tank-raised and are considered good for saltwater aquariums. The common clownfish (also called the clown-anemonefish), which features the classic orange-and-white stripes, is the most popular species. Clark's clownfish looks similar to the common clownfish, and is known for being hardy—that is, strong and tough. Other popular species include the saddleback clownfish, the maroon clownfish, the percula clownfish, and the cinnamon clownfish.

The orange-fin clownfish

The cinnamon clownfish

The white-maned clownfish

What Should You Look for When Choosing a Clownfish?

Before purchasing a clownfish, your family should research different species and make a list of ones that match your family's skill level and interests. Also, determine how many clownfish you wish to buy. Many experts suggest purchasing a mated pair (a male and a female).

Once you have decided what kind of clownfish you would like, look for a responsible dealer who sells marine fish. Many dealers sell tank-raised clownfish, which helps prevent wild clownfish and their habitats from being harmed. Never buy wild clownfish unless they have been certified (approved) by the Marine Aquarium Council (MAC). The dealer should be glad to tell you where the fish came from.

If possible, buy your fish from a local store rather than by mail order. At a store, you can see what the fish look like and how they behave. A healthy clownfish should look lively, brightly colored, and alert. Avoid fish that have dull colors, drooping fins, or are breathing heavily, which may be signs of illness.

Tank-raised clownfish are often healthier than pet fish that are captured in the wild.

What Does a Clownfish Eat?

Clownfish eat both plant matter and seafood, so they are said to be omnivores *(OM nuh vawrs)*. Giving your pet clownfish a variety of foods will help to keep it healthy. This might include pellet or flake fish food formulated for saltwater fish, freeze-dried krill, fresh or frozen brine shrimp, and zooplankton (tiny sea animals). The algae growing in the tank should supply all the plant matter your clownfish needs. Follow the instructions on the packages for rehydrating dried items or thawing frozen ones before feeding.

Feed your clownfish in the morning and the evening. Slowly sprinkle in as much as they will eat in about five minutes. After one or two hours, use a net to scoop any leftovers out of the water.

Clownfish eat small animals
near their anemone host.

Where Should a Pet Clownfish Be Kept?

Your fish must be kept in a saltwater aquarium outfitted with the equipment needed to keep the water clean, warm, and with plenty of oxygen. Your family will also need equipment to check the level of salt and other substances. Listed below are a few pieces of equipment that every saltwater aquarium needs:

- glass tank (at least 30 gallons or 113.6 liters for two fish)
- tank cover
- water heater
- water filters
- air pump
- fluorescent lights
- hydrometer (read about this on page 28)
- thermometer
- prepackaged salt mix

Glass tanks can be very expensive and go up in price with size, but it is essential that your tank be large enough for the number of animals living in it.

A saltwater aquarium

How Do You Make a Nice Home for Your Clownfish?

When designing spaces inside the aquarium, try to recreate a clownfish's coral reef environment. For fish-only tanks, you can get models of coral. (Real coral must be carefully cleaned and may have been harvested illegally, so it is not recommended for your tank.) Arrange the coral pieces in ways that provide different nooks and crannies where your clownfish can hide.

You will need to cover the bottom of your tank with gravel. Coral gravel or crushed oyster shell are two good choices for marine aquariums. You can also ask your dealer for other recommendations.

After about a week, you may notice a slimy green substance called algae growing on the coral. Algae is a plantlike organism that clownfish like to eat. It is best to leave the algae on the coral, though you may remove it from the tank glass. To prevent algae from growing uncontrollably, keep a snail in the tank. Snails are big algae-eaters.

Clownfish like having places to hide and things to swim around.

What Else Can Be Added to Saltwater Aquariums?

A clownfish's natural habitat is filled with many different kinds of invertebrates (animals without backbones), including anemones, corals, sponges, and sea urchins. Some people add these animals to their aquariums to try to recreate a clownfish's coral reef habitat. In fact, clownfish are happiest when they have anemones in the tank. However, reef aquariums are very difficult to maintain and are recommended only for expert marine aquarium keepers. For the less experienced marine aquarists, a fish-only tank is best.

Clownfish can live peacefully in a tank with certain kinds of fish, but make sure your family has had time to learn how to keep your fish healthy and happy before taking this next step. You must consider several things, such as how large your tank is, how big the fish will get, what it eats, and whether the fish is aggressive toward other fish. If your family wishes to add different fish to your tank, ask your dealer for recommendations.

Clownfish and their anemone host

What Daily Care Is Needed?

Several kinds of daily care are needed for clownfish and their aquarium:

- Feed your fish twice a day, and remove any uneaten food. Also, observe your fish for any signs of illness. Clownfish should be alert and eager to eat. A lack of appetite may mean your fish is sick.

- The aquarium lights should be turned on for 10 to 12 hours each day, with 14 to 12 hours of darkness. You can purchase an automatic timer for your lights to ensure the appropriate day-night cycle.

- The water temperature should stay between 75 and 80 °F (24 and 27 °C). Check the tank thermometer and adjust the heater if necessary.

- You must also check the water level in the tank every day. If you notice the level has lowered, add purified fresh water—NOT salt water. When water in the tank evaporates (changes from a liquid to a gas), the salt stays in the tank. Adding fresh water will help balance the level of salt.

A water filter

How Important Is Water Quality?

Keeping the right chemical balance in the aquarium is essential to your clownfish's survival. A young adult or adult should perform regular tests to ensure the chemical balance of the water is suitable for your fish.

Prepackaged sea salt mixes are available at most pet stores. Follow the instructions to mix the correct amount of sea salt with purified water. Your family may want to store prepared salt water in a cool, dry place for when you need to replace the tank water.

A device called a hydrometer *(hy DROM uh tuhr)* will allow you to measure salt levels in the aquarium. Your family will also need to do other chemistry tests, such as measuring pH and the levels of ammonia, nitrites, and nitrates. Each of these elements must be at just the right level to keep your clownfish happy and healthy. The water should be tested every day for the first two to three months and every one to two weeks once the tank is established. Your dealer should be able to recommend test kits.

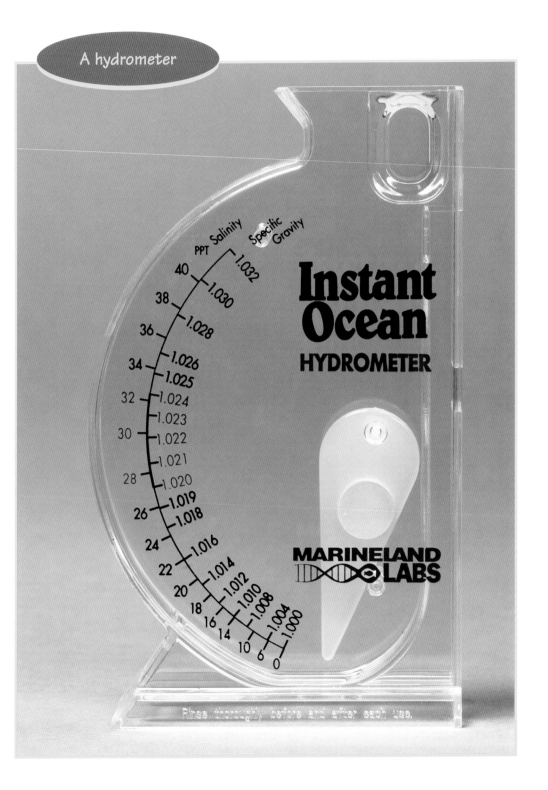

A hydrometer

How Do You Keep a Saltwater Aquarium Clean?

A messy bedroom might not be a big deal, but a dirty aquarium is a life-or-death matter for fish. Because of this, saltwater aquariums should be cleaned often. Aquarium water can be contaminated with harmful salmonella bacteria, so only an adult or young adult should handle cleaning the tank.

The aquarium glass should be scrubbed once a week. Every two to four weeks, the filters in the tank should be cleaned and wastes removed from the gravel on the tank floor. Pet stores sell special vacuums for this process.

Every week or two, about 10 to 20 percent of the water should be removed and replaced with prepared salt water. Many people use a long hose and a bucket to remove the water, but pet stores also sell other kinds of equipment for this task. Experts recommend replacing half of the water if your tests show there is a problem or if your fish look sick or upset.

Always wash your hands if you touch aquarium water or anything that's been inside the tank.

How Do Clownfish Breed?

Interestingly, all clownfish begin life as males. As they mature, the largest fish in a small group becomes a female who can lay eggs. The second biggest fish becomes a male who can fertilize the eggs—the others cannot. If the female dies, the breeding male becomes the female, and the next biggest fish takes his place.

A female clownfish lays her eggs on a surface, such as a rock. The male fertilizes and guards the eggs, fanning them with his tail to give them oxygen. The eggs start out orange and become see-through until the babies' eyes are visible. They hatch in 6 to 15 days, always in the dark.

A mated pair of clownfish

How Can You Help Care for Clownfish Young?

A comfortably settled mated pair of clownfish will often spawn (lay and fertilize eggs) in an aquarium. Raising the young is complicated, though. For that, your family will need a separate tank with plenty of oxygen and heat.

Some people move the eggs to a separate tank just before hatching; others wait until right afterward. Newly hatched fish, or larvae, need live food. Start with rotifers (dust-speck-sized aquatic creatures). After five days, feed them brine shrimp. Do not worry if many of the little fish die—that happens in nature, too. You have done a terrific job if even a few survive.

After about three months, find the fish new homes in pairs or as singles. Adult clownfish become aggressive toward one another in large groups.

Clownfish larvae

35

What Are Some Other Kinds of Saltwater Aquarium Fish?

There are hundreds of different kinds of saltwater aquarium fish. Some are quite difficult to care for and are best left to experienced marine aquarists. Beginners have a lot to choose from, though. Remember to buy tank-raised fish whenever possible.

Damselfish, which belong to the same family as clownfish, are popular because they are hardy. The blue reef chromis, a shiny blue damselfish, likes to swim in shoals, or schools.

Cardinalfish are known for being slow-moving and calm. The different species come in impressive colors: fiery red flamefish; polka-dot-tailed pajamafish; candy-striped cardinalfish with stripes running nose to tail; and long-finned, vertically striped Banggai cardinalfish.

More fish suitable for a saltwater aquarium are described on the following pages.

A cocoa damselfish

What Is a Valentini Sharpnosed Puffer?

Puffers are fish that can inflate their bodies like a balloon when they are angry or surprised. Most species of puffers grow too large and are too aggressive to do well in an average-sized aquarium, but the Valentini sharpnosed puffer stays small—around 4 inches (10 centimeters) long. This pretty, spotted-and-striped fish is known by several names, including "Valentini toby" and "black-saddled toby." Its scientific name is *Canthigaster valentini,* and it is found in the Indian Ocean from the eastern coastline of Africa to Australia.

Spotted sharpnosed puffers usually do not bother other kinds of fish, though they will eat invertebrates and may be aggressive toward other puffers. It is best to keep one puffer at a time in a fish-only aquarium.

A Valentini sharpnosed puffer

What Is a Hawkfish?

Hawkfish are small fish that live in coral reefs. Unlike most fish, they do not have the inflatable organ called a swim bladder, which allows fish to float. Instead of floating, hawkfish use their fins to perch upon coral so they can keep an eye on their surroundings. You may notice an aquarium hawkfish observing your movements, too.

Hawkfish got their name because they swoop down on their food catch, much like hawks. They are known as one of the easier marine aquarium fish to care for, though they are better for fish-only tanks.

Most hawkfish grow between 3 and 5 inches (7.6 and 12.7 centimeters) long, but some grow as long as 12 inches (30 centimeters). Two popular types are the flame hawkfish, which is bright red with black markings, and the longnosed hawkfish, which has a pattern of orange-and-white squares on its body and a pointy snout.

A longnosed hawkfish

41

What Is a Goby?

Gobies are bottom-dwelling fish that live mostly in the shallow parts of warm oceans. There are about 2,000 different species of gobies, and they come in an amazing variety of colors. Most gobies are only about 1 to 5 inches (2½ to 13 centimeters) long, though a few kinds grow to 1 foot (30 centimeters).

Gobies devote themselves to cleaning their surroundings—including fellow fish. Some gobies establish "cleaning stations," where larger fish line up and wait for the gobies to eat harmful parasites off their bodies.

Many species of gobies are suitable for beginning marine aquarists. One popular kind is the tiny neon goby, about 2 inches (5 centimeters) long with a glowing blue stripe. Randall's watchman goby (also called Randall's shrimp goby) forms a special relationship with a certain kind of shrimp in the wild. In exchange for sharing the shrimp's burrow, the goby watches for predators (hunting animals) and warns the shrimp when they are near. This kind of goby may burrow in the gravel at the bottom of the tank.

A goby

What Is a Dottyback?

Dottybacks are shy fish that often hide among the caves and crevices in coral reefs. They are usually about 3 inches (7.6 centimeters) long, and many species are available tank-raised. They come in an amazing variety of colors, as you can tell from the names of a few popular ones: the neon dottyback, magenta dottyback, orchid dottyback, and sunrise dottyback.

Dottybacks are often good for beginning marine aquarists. However, most dottybacks are territorial, which makes them aggressive under some conditions. It is best not to have more than one dottyback in a tank unless the tank is large enough to give each fish some space. It also helps if the dottyback is smaller than the other fish in the tank.

A magenta dottyback

45

What Is a Mandarinfish?

Mandarinfish are tropical fish that live in the coral reefs of the western Pacific Ocean. They are popular with experienced aquarists for their beautiful colors and patterns. Mandarinfish may have been named for the brightly colored silk Mandarin Chinese robes of the 1800's.

Mandarinfish are small, peaceful, bottom-dwelling fish. They typically are only 2½ inches (6 centimeters) long or smaller, which can make them difficult to spot in their reef habitat. When they swim, they look a bit like tiny helicopters. They move very slowly, using their fins to hover above the coral or ocean floor as they search for food.

Mandarinfish have very specific dietary needs, so they are recommended only for expert aquarists.

A mandarinfish

How Long Do Clownfish Live?

It is difficult to say how long clownfish live since so many factors affect this. Of course, you cannot know how old a wild-caught fish is when you buy it—another reason to get tank-raised fish.

Generally, clownfish have a longer life span than other saltwater aquarium fish, many of which live only about 2 to 4 years. Assuming a clownfish lives in a smoothly running aquarium, it may live between 4 and 10 years.

Some aquarists report having clownfish that are much older than the upper estimate. In addition, a 2006 study found that the percula clownfish in a New Guinea lagoon may be 30 years old.

Some clownfish live
for several years.

How Does a Clownfish Sense Its Surroundings?

Fish have the same senses you do—they can see, hear, smell, taste, and touch. They also have a sensory organ (body part) unlike anything people have. It is called the lateral line, and it helps fish sense changes in the movement of water.

Clownfish use their senses in many different ways. Scientists believe that clownfish larvae use their sense of smell to find their way back to the coral reefs where they were born. In the wild, after clownfish hatch from their eggs, the sea carries the tiny larvae into the open waters. Later, if they are lucky enough to grow up, the larvae swim back to the reef.

Clownfish use hearing, too. They make chirping and popping noises to scare predators and to communicate with one another. Their sense of sight is also important. Aquarium keepers whose clownfish become blind because of disease report that when the fish cannot see food, they stop eating.

Clownfish make chirping
noises to communicate
with each other.

How Are Clownfish Protected Against an Anemone's Sting?

Clownfish are one of the only fish species that is not harmed by a sea anemone's sting. But clownfish are not born with this protection. They develop their immunity (resistance) to an anemone's sting over time.

Once a young clownfish has chosen its host anemone, it does a kind of dance to expose itself gradually to the anemone and prepare the layer of mucus that provides protection from the stings. Over several days, the clownfish slowly increases the amount of time it spends in the anemone's tentacles. During this time, the anemone's stinging cells mix with the clownfish's slimy coating.

Once a clownfish's mucus is completely mixed with the anemone's cells, it has the same dangerous mucus as its host.

Clownfish and their
anemone host

Are Wild Clownfish Endangered?

Clownfish are not endangered, but they depend on their coral reef habitats. Tragically, coral reefs throughout the world are seriously endangered by pollution (human-made wastes) and other human activities—including gathering fish and corals for pet stores. If these habitats disappear, so may the clownfish and thousands of species of fish and other animals that depend on them.

Though clownfish are not endangered, the number of wild clownfish has dropped drastically in the past 10 years. This is partly because people are catching more wild clownfish to meet the growing demand of the pet trade. In 2003, an animated Disney movie called *Finding Nemo,* which starred a talking clownfish, became a box office hit. Some experts believe that *Finding Nemo's* popularity could have caused more people to want clownfish as pets, even though the movie was about Nemo's struggle to escape his aquarium and make it back home to his coral reef.

Finding Nemo was a popular Disney movie.

What Are Some Common Signs of Illness in Clownfish?

Observe your fish carefully every day for signs of illness. A healthy fish should have clear, alert eyes. Its skin and fins should be smooth, without bumps or broken areas, and its mouth should not hang open. It should swim upright in the water.

Common signs of illness include a lack of appetite, unusually fast breathing, abnormal swimming behavior, lack of movement, and rubbing or twitching of the body or fins. Other symptoms include abnormal or dull coloration, white spots, cloudy eyes, and holes or lesions on the body.

Health problems are often caused by harmful parasites, which are more likely to be carried in on wild-caught fish than tank-raised ones. Saltwater, or marine, ich *(IHK)* is common; it shows up as white spots on the skin. Clownfish are especially vulnerable to a parasitic protozoan, *Brooklynella hostilis.* In fact, the infestation is sometimes called clownfish disease.

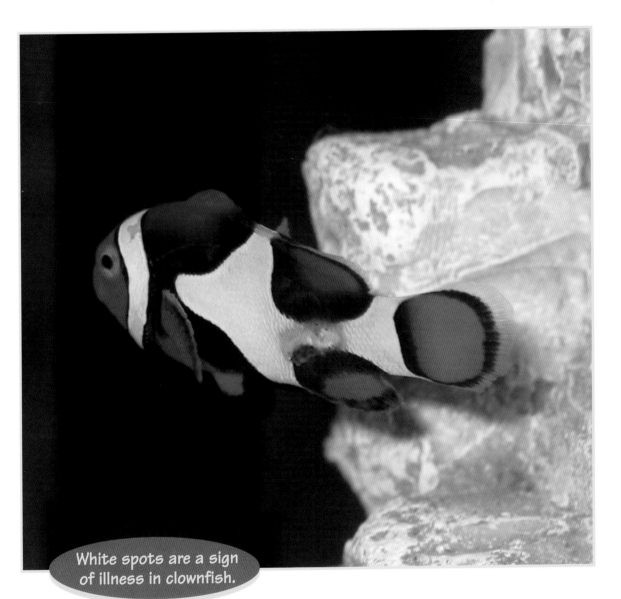

White spots are a sign
of illness in clownfish.

How Do You Care for a Sick Pet Fish?

If your clownfish gets sick, move it to a separate tank—this is called quarantining. With luck, you will prevent its aquarium mates from getting sick, too. Usually, treatment involves adding chemicals to the water in the tank, or changing the salt content of the water. You might also briefly "dip" the fish in a specially treated water, then return it to the regular salt water.

Fish do not need to have regular visits to a veterinarian but, if they get sick, it is ideal to get a doctor's advice. Not all veterinarians are trained to treat fish. See if you can find one in your area. If not, your family can try consulting staff at a zoo, city aquarium, or good pet store.

At the first sign of illness,
move a sick fish to a
separate tank.

What Are Your Responsibilities as an Owner?

Before you take on the responsibilities of keeping a saltwater aquarium, you should understand that it is a big commitment. The creatures in your tank depend completely on you and your family for survival. You must learn how to set up the tank and keep all the equipment in good working order. Your family members will need to share the work of cleaning the aquarium, feeding the fish and monitoring their health, and providing any necessary medical treatment.

Enthusiastic aquarium keepers often feel that their fish have engaging personalities. Still, fish and invertebrate animals are not cuddly like dogs and cats. The appeal of an aquarium is really about observing and appreciating the fascinating underwater world you have created.

Observing a saltwater aquarium

Saltwater Aquarium Fish Fun Facts

→ Clownfish are fiercely protective of their anemone hosts. Some have even chased and bitten at divers who get too close!

→ Scientists have studied clownfish to develop a skin lotion that protects people from jellyfish stings. The product coats the skin, much the way a clownfish's mucus protects it from an anemone's sting.

→ Leafy seadragons and weedy seadragons look just like floating pieces of seaweed in the water—unless you take a really close look. Then you will see that they have heads like seahorses and pipefish, to which they are related.

→ The shortest-lived vertebrate animal known is the coral reef pygmy goby. It goes from egg to old age in less than 60 days!

Leafy seadragon

Glossary

alga A simple organism that lives in water or moist soil.

colony A group of animals or plants of the same kind, living or growing together.

coral The skeleton formed by tiny sea animals massed together.

gill A feathery, blood-filled organ that some animals use to take in oxygen from the surrounding water.

habitat Where an animal lives.

invertebrate An animal without a backbone.

larvae Animals, such as fish or frogs, that have just hatched from eggs and whose bodies will go through major changes before they take on their adult form.

omnivore An animal that eats both animals and plants.

parasite An organism (living creature) that feeds on and lives on or in the body of another organism, often causing harm to the being on which it feeds.

predator An animal that hunts other animals for food.

reef A mass of coral that rises close to the surface of the water.

sea anemone A kind of sea animal that resembles a flowering plant.

spawn To produce or fertilize eggs in a watery environment.

species A group of animals that have certain permanent characteristics in common and are able to produce offspring.

tank raised Fish or other water animals that are bred and raised by people.

tentacle The narrow, flexible body part that certain animals use for feeling, grasping, or feeding.

tropical An area of Earth that is near the equator.

Index (**Boldface** indicates a photo, map, or illustration.)

For more information about clownfish and other saltwater aquarium fish, try these resources:

Books:
An Essential Guide to Choosing Your Marine Tropical Fish by Dick Mills (Barron's, 2001)

Marine Aquariums: Basic Setup and Maintenance by Ray Hunziker (Bowtie Press, 2005)

Your First Marine Aquarium by John H. Tullock (Barron's, 2006)

Web sites:
Clownfish Database
http://clownfish.webreefs.com

Marine Aquarium Council
www.aquariumcouncil.org

Monterey Bay Aquarium
http://www.montereybayaquarium.org/

National Geographic: Fish
http://animals.nationalgeographic.com/animals/fish.html

Clownfish Classification

Scientists classify animals by placing them into groups. The animal kingdom is a group that contains all the world's animals. Phylum, class, order, and family are smaller groups. Each phylum contains many classes. A class contains orders, an order contains families, and a family contains genuses. One or more species belong to each genus. Each species has its own scientific name. Here is how the animals in this book fit into this system.

Animals with backbones and their relatives (Phylum Chordata)
Bony fish (Class Osteichthyes)
Ray-finned fish (Subclass Actinopterygii)
"Perchlike" fish (Order Perciformes)

Clownfish and their damselfish relatives (Family Pomacentridae)

Common clownfish	*Amphiprion ocellaris*
Percula clownfish	*Amphiprion percula*
Clark's clownfish	*Amphiprion clarkii*
Tomato clownfish	*Amphiprion frenatus*
Pink skunk clownfish	*Amphiprion perideraion*
Blue reef chromis	*Chromis cyanea*

Other saltwater aquarium fish

Lionfish	Scorpaenidae family
Porcupinefish	Diodontidae family
Parrotfish	Scaridae family
Moray eels	Muraenidae family
Pipefish	Syngnathidae family
Seahorses	*Hippocampus spp.*
Pajamafish (cardinalfish)	*Sphaeramia nematoptera*
Banggai cardinalfish	*Pterapogon kauderni*
Flamefish (cardinalfish)	*Apogon maculatus*
Valenti sharpnosed puffer	*Canthigaster valenti*
Flame hawkfish	*Neocirrhitus armatus*
Longnosed hawkfish	*Oxycirrhites typus*
Neon goby	*Gobiosoma oceanops* (and other spp.)
Randall's watchman goby	*Amblyeleotris randalli*
Blennies	Blenniidae family
Neon dottyback	*Pseudochromis aldabraensis*
Magenta dottyback	*Pseudochromis porphyreus*
Orchid dottyback	*Pseudochromis fridmani*
Sunrise dottyback	*Pseudochromis flavivertex*
Leafy seadragon	*Phycodurus eques*
Weedy seadragon	*Phyllopteryx taeniolatus*
Coral reef pygmy goby	*Eviota sigillata*
Mandarinfish	Callionymidae family